INDIANA
impressions

photography by Richard Fields

FARCOUNTRY
PRESS

Above: Morel mushrooms, a favorite of wild-mushroom hunters, can be found in April and May in Indiana's forests—and, sometimes, even in lawns!

Right: Canoeing on Sugar Creek in Turkey Run State Park in western Indiana, near Marshall.

Front cover: Tulip tree leaves and flower, Indiana's state tree since 1931.

Back cover: The Soldiers' and Sailors' Monument in the center of Indianapolis defines Monument Circle. Designed by Bruno Schmitz (a German architect), it was built in 1888–1901 to honor Indiana's military men in the Civil War and previous wars.

Title page: Basketball and Indiana are practically synonymous.

ISBN 1-56037-296-6
Photography © 2005 by Richard Fields
© 2005 Farcountry Press

For more information on our books write Farcountry Press, P.O. Box 5630, Helena, MT 59604; call (800) 821-3874; or visit www.farcountrypress.com.

Created, produced, and designed in the United States. Printed in China.
09 08 07 06 05   1 2 3 4 5

Left: The world-famous Indy 500 has run annually (except during World Wars I and II) since 1911.

Below: These Hoosier-brand tires are ready for use in the Brickyard 400 race, held at the Indianapolis Motor Speedway since 1994. The race is named for the second surface of the 2.5-mile oval raceway: 3.2 million bricks, laid in 1909.

Right: Actor James Dean's grave (with kiss marks) in Fairmount. Born in Marion, he moved to Los Angeles when he was five, returning to Fairmount to live with his aunt and uncle after his mother died. The town is also home of the James Dean Memorial Gallery museum and many other significant Dean sites.

Below: The NCAA (National Collegiate Athletic Association) has been headquartered in Indianapolis since 2000. Both the office building and the Hall of Champions are in White River State Park.

Above: Ernie Pyle State Historic Site honors the famous World War II journalist, who was born on a farm southwest of Dana. This historic house was moved from the farm to Dana. The site includes two Quonset huts with World War II exhibits.

Right: The peony replaced the zinnia as Indiana's state flower in 1957.
PHOTO BY RICHARD DAY

Left: The boardwalk at Twin Swamps Nature Preserve in Posey County, southern Indiana. Set aside in 1987, the preserve helps sustain one of the state's last stands of bald cypress trees, a relative of redwoods and sequoias.

Below: Great blue heron at Potato Creek State Park in northern Indiana.

Right: Wyandotte Cave is open May 1 through Labor Day for public tours; it is closed during the fall and winter to protect the bat population during their hibernation. It is the third largest hibernaculum for Indiana bats in the state, with almost ten percent of the state's bat population using it. Since the 1980s, numbers have steadily increased from as few as 200 individuals. The companion Silberts Cave is open March 1 through October 31.

Far right: Green's Bluff Nature Preserve in Owen County shows beautiful fall foliage, an attraction that draws many people to Indiana in October.

Above: The entry gate to West Baden Springs, a national historic landmark in southern Indiana near French Lick. This health spa and resort hotel was built in 1902 and has been partially restored with a formal garden, 100-by-200-foot domed atrium, pavilions, and first-floor rooms. Al Capone was once a guest here, as well as many high-society and political figures from the early twentieth century.

Left: On the banks of the Ohio River near Clarksville, the Falls of the Ohio State Park shows a dramatic riverscape at dusk.

Right: The Indianapolis Colts play the San Francisco '49ers in RCA Dome in Indianapolis. The Colts moved to Indianapolis from Baltimore the same year that the RCA Dome was built: 1984.

Below: John Deere is a familiar name in the state fair's tractor parade!

Left: A tobacco field in Switzerland County, southeastern part of the state.

Below: The eastern pondhawk, shown below on a blade of grass, is one of 97 species of dragonflies found in Indiana.

Left: Cross-country skiers at Lake James, in northeastern Indiana.

Below: If you travel north out of West Fork, in the middle of the Hoosier National Forest, you'll find Hemlock Cliffs. This beautiful valley has some unique trees and plants and sandstone rock formations. Pictured here are large, seasonal ice formations.

Above: A quarter-mile toboggan track shoots through Pokagon State Park.

Above: Male cardinal, Indiana's state bird since 1933. PHOTO BY RICHARD DAY

Right: Mill Creek plunges 20 feet down Upper Cataract Falls and 18 feet down Lower Cataract Falls, pictured here. The creek drops 80 feet total down the two falls and the cascades that precede them. The double falls, unequalled in size in the state, are near Cataract in northern Owen County, western Indiana.

Left: Rail fence at Conner Prairie, an open-air living-history museum in central Indiana that encompasses five historic areas on 1,400 acres.

Right and below: Parke County invites visitors to a slower time in history. Shown here is maple sap being tapped and processed into syrup, as demonstrated in a "sugar shack" featured on the Maple Syrup Festival tour.

Above: The rich glow of maple leaves in autumn brings warmth to the landscape.

Right: Fishing boat at sunset on Lake Michigan, near Michigan City.

Above: Indiana's only Civil War battle site was in the state's first capital city, Corydon, near the Kentucky border.

Left: Civil War re-enactors at Billie Creek Village, a re-created early 1900s burg in western Indiana near Rockville.

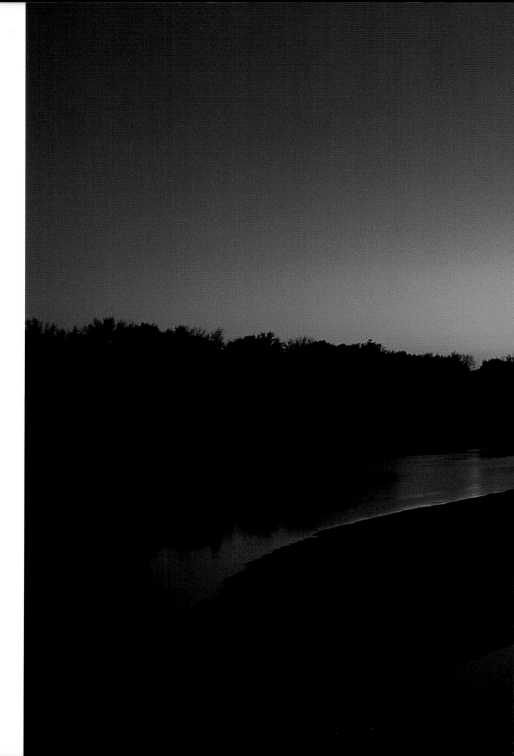

The beauty of moonlight on Indiana's most famous river, the Wabash, makes evident why the state song is "On the Banks of the Wabash, Far Away," by Paul Dresser. The waterway passes through two-thirds of Indiana's counties, entering the state on the Ohio border near New Corydon and flowing west to meet the Ohio River below Mount Vernon. All but thirty miles of the river are in Indiana. The name derives from the Miami Indian word "Wah-Bah Shik-Ki," meaning pure white.

Facing page: Nashville is famous as an artists' colony and as a gateway into Brown County State Park, Indiana's largest.

Right and below: In-state rivalry between Indiana's two largest universities, Indiana and Purdue, gets especially hot when they meet for sporting events.

Above: Redbud and dogwood blossoms brighten spring!

Left: This lighthouse on Lake Michigan near Michigan City
was constructed in 1904.

Right: Members of the Amish community participate in a barn-raising in Daviess County.

Far right: Indiana has three major ports, two on the Ohio River and one on Lake Michigan. Burns Harbor is in Portage.

Left: Indiana State House in Indianapolis.

Below: This *Madonna of the Trail* sculpture in Richmond, by August Leimbach, is one of twelve erected to mark the National Old Trails Road where it passed through each state. Indiana's was dedicated on October 28, 1928.

MADONNA OF THE TRAIL

Above: The "roofless church" in New Harmony is an architectural landmark designed by Philip Johnson and built in 1960. The site of two of America's great utopian communities in the early 1800s, the town of New Harmony has a long spiritual history.

Above: Fishing on Syracuse Lake in northern Indiana.

Left: The marina at Lake Wawasee, Indiana's largest natural lake, near Syracuse.

Right: Limestone pothole formations at Falls of the Ohio State Park, known for its Devonian fossil beds.

Below: Crevice Rock, Turkey Run State Park.

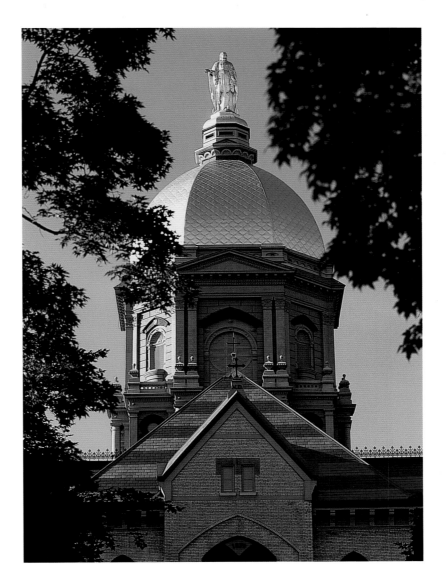

Above: Main Building at Notre Dame University, in South Bend.

Left: The 72,000-square-foot Indiana State Museum in Indianapolis was built from Indiana materials—limestone, sandstone, steel, brick, and glass.

Above: Detail at the Bybee Stone Company, a limestone mill in Elletsville. Bybee limestone was used to rebuild the Pentagon following the attacks on September 11, 2001.

Right: Aerial photograph of a limestone quarry in Monroe County.

Far right: Grissom Air Museum near Peru gives visitors an insider's look at aviation history from WW II through today.

PASSIONATE PAULETTE

B-25J BOMBER
·Speed..285 mph · Span..67ft 7 in · Length..53 ft 6 in

Most widely used Bomber during World War II. The
B-25 was used for both High and Low Level Bombing,
Strafing, Photo Reconnaissance, Submarine Patrol, and
as a Fighter. The B-25H was the most heavily armed
aircraft during the war, carrying a 75mm Cannon and
14 · 50 caliber Machine Guns. More than 9,800 B-25's
were built. On April
Doolittle success
for the United St
B-25 was used i

USA

**Please
Stay Behind
The Rope**

The Wind Beneath These Wings!

Adopt-a-Plane   Sponsorship
Program   Program

Basic care and cleaning Financial support for the
of this aircraft   preservation of this
provided by   aircraft provided by

Students of Vincennes University
Aviation Technology Center at
Indianapolis International Airport

Left: Path through Oakhurst Gardens, part of the Minnetrista Cultural Center, located on the banks of the White River in Muncie. Opened in 1988, the center preserves the cultural heritage of the region.

Facing page: It seems everyone in Indiana picks up a basketball at some point—and the younger, the better!

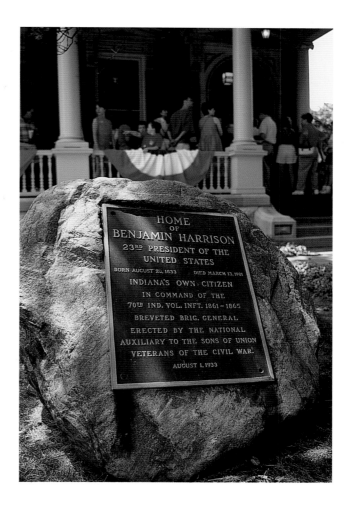

Above: The twenty-third president of the United States, Benjamin Harrison was inaugurated 100 years after George Washington and served from 1889 to 1893. His home in Indianapolis is a national registered landmark.

Left: Horse-drawn boat rides are offered along the Whitewater Canal, a state historic site, in Metamora.

More than 10,000 migrating sandhill cranes use Jasper-Pulaski Fish and Wildlife Area in northern Indiana. Sunrise and sunset in late September through December are the best viewing times; crane numbers peak in mid-November.

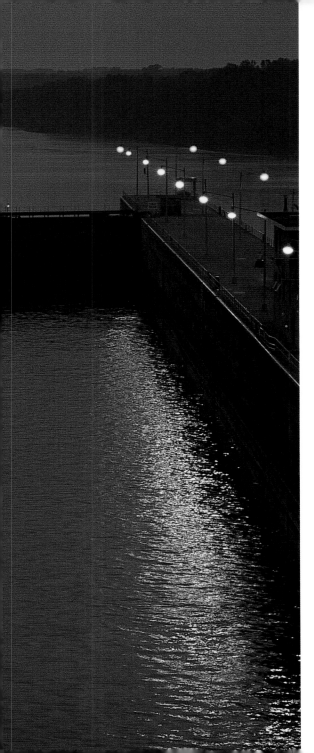

Left: Locks and dam on the Ohio River at Uniontown, Perry County. Waterways are an important mode of commercial transportation in Indiana.

Below: This one-of-a-kind 1934 Bendix is on display at the Studebaker Museum in South Bend, along with over seventy other vintage vehicles spanning America's history from the Conestoga wagons to high performance cars.

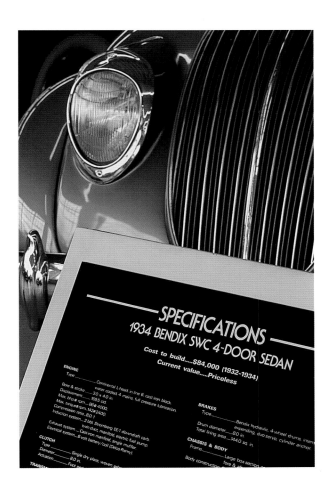

Above: Indiana is a major producer of tomatoes for processing in the U.S. These cherry tomatoes at the Bloomington farmers' market, however, are destined for someone's salad!

Right: Dunbar Bridge in Putnam County is one of more than ninety covered bridges still left in the state; there were once an estimated 400 to 500.

Left: Kayaker in whitewater, St. Joseph's River, South Bend. Within the city limits, an artificial kayak raceway was built for world-class training and competition.

Far left: The annual summer Madison Regatta on the Ohio River is a hydroplane boat race where speeds reach over 200 mph.

Right: The nonprofit Minnetrista Cultural Center serves seven counties in east central Indiana.

Below: Angel Mound State Historical Site near Evansville preserves a settlement of the Middle Mississippian Native American culture that was abandoned for unknown reasons about A.D. 1450. At its height, nearly 3,000 people occupied the town.

Left: Fort Quiatenon Historic Park near West Lafayette hosts an autumn Feast of the Hunters' Moon each year to recreate the historic annual gathering of French fur traders and Native Americans on the banks of the Wabash River.

Far left: The Lincoln Museum in Fort Wayne is the largest museum in the world dedicated to Abraham Lincoln. Programs include a permanent exhibit and a research library with more than 300 original documents.

Above: Clifty Falls State Park, with its 60-foot waterfall and steep-sided canyon walls, offers hikes through beautiful and intimate landscapes.

Right: One of the many lush landscapes seen at the Foellinger-Freimann Botanical Conservatory, owned and operated by the Fort Wayne Parks and Recreation Department.

Left: The large spring that rises in Orangeville is actually the reappearance of the Lost River, which disappears underground southeast of Orleans.

Right and below: Wine production is a growing industry in Indiana; many wineries offer wine-tasting facilities and other amenities.

Right: Monroe County Courthouse in Bloomington was dedicated in 1908. It has a fish weathervane that came from the 1827 courthouse.

Below: The "World's Largest Christmas Tree" is formed each year on Thanksgiving weekend by stringing lights on the Soldiers' and Sailors' Monument on the Circle in Indianapolis.

Left: Peru, Indiana, served as winter quarters for many circuses until the 1940s. Now it is home to the Circus Hall of Fame.

Far left: Rose Hulman (formerly Rose Polytechnic) students with a solar car they built for Sunrayce, a race from Indianapolis to Golden, Colorado.

Right: Indiana Dunes State Park on Lake Michigan offers 3 miles of beach and sand dunes—a unique environment. It is part of a larger Indiana Dunes National Lakeshore, which runs for nearly 25 miles and is ranked seventh among national parks for native plant diversity.

Below: Sandhill cranes in snow, Jasper-Pulaski Fish and Wildlife Area, northern Indiana.

Left: Fishing at the Falls of the Ohio State Park.

Far left: Corn stalks backlit by a setting sun: you can almost hear the crickets, smell the sweetness.

Above: The tulip tree (yellow poplar) is a fast-growing shade tree that provides food for many animals. According to legend, Daniel Boone favored this hardwood for his canoes.

Right: Rows and rows of corn. Indiana is the fifth-largest national producer of corn for grain and ranks seventeenth for sweet corn.

Far right: Stone arch bridge in McCormick's Creek State Park, Indiana's first. Near Spencer, it is known for limestone, thick woods, and water features.

Right: In 1991, an
American Institute of
Architects survey ranked
Columbus sixth among
all U.S. cities for its
world-class architecture.

Far right: Skyline of the
state capital, Indianapolis.

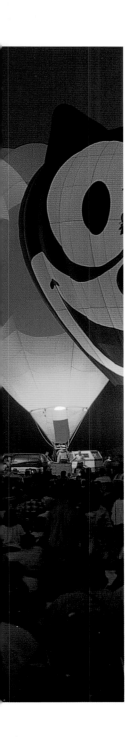

Above: Indiana University's Goethe-Link Observatory.

Left: Hot-air balloons light up like jack-o'-lanterns at night during the Marshall County Blueberry Festival in northern Indiana, held on Labor Day weekend.

Richard Fields is the head photographer for the Indiana Department of Natural Resources and *Outdoor Indiana* magazine. Other works include *Indiana from the Air,* published by Indiana University Press. His work has also been featured in numerous other natural history publications, including Sierra Club calendars, National Geographic books, and *National Wildlife, Audubon, Outside,* and *Nature Conservancy* magazines. He is a contributor to *The Natural Heritage of Indiana* and the *Indiana Wildlife Viewing Guide.*

Richard was raised in Kokomo, Indiana, where he began experimenting with photography using attic and basement darkrooms in the late 1960s. Self-taught, he has studied briefly under Wil Counts, Bing Davis, Bill Thomas, John Shaw, and Larry West. He graduated in 1981 from Purdue University with a degree in natural resources and environmental science; he began his career with the Indiana DNR and *Outdoor Indiana* magazine in 1985.

Richard makes his home in Spencer, Indiana, where he lives with his wife, two teenage sons, three cats, and one axolotl.